How Engineers Find Solutions

Robin Johnson
Crabtree Publishing Company
www.crabtreebooks.com

Author
Robin Johnson

Publishing plan research and development:
Reagan Miller

Editor
Crystal Sikkens

Proofreader
Kathy Middleton

Photo research
Samara Parent
Crystal Sikkens

Design
Samara Parent

**Production coordinator
and prepress technician**
Samara Parent

Print coordinator
Margaret Amy Salter

Photographs
© Hero Images Inc. / Alamy: pages 14, 15
Thinkstock: front cover (left), pages 1 (kids), 4,
    7 (bottom middle), 8 (girls)
All other images by Shutterstock

Library and Archives Canada Cataloguing in Publication

Johnson, Robin (Robin R.), author
        How engineers find solutions / Robin Johnson.

(Engineering close-up)
Includes index.
Issued in print and electronic formats.
ISBN 978-0-7787-0095-1 (bound).--ISBN 978-0-7787-0113-2 (pbk.).--
ISBN 978-1-4271-9402-2 (html).--ISBN 978-1-4271-9406-0 (pdf)

        1. Engineers--Juvenile literature. I. Title.

QC225.5.J64 2014   j534   C2014-900805-8
                                        C2014-900806-6

Library of Congress Cataloging-in-Publication Data

CIP available at Library of Congress

Crabtree Publishing Company

Printed in Canada/032014/BF20140212

www.crabtreebooks.com   1-800-387-7650

**Published in Canada
Crabtree Publishing**
616 Welland Ave.
St. Catharines, Ontario
L2M 5V6

**Published in the United States
Crabtree Publishing**
PMB 59051
350 Fifth Avenue, 59th Floor
New York, New York 10118

**Published in the United Kingdom
Crabtree Publishing**
Maritime House
Basin Road North, Hove
BN41 1WR

**Published in Australia
Crabtree Publishing**
3 Charles Street
Coburg North
VIC 3058

Contents

Making a plan

Have you ever made a sand castle at the beach? If you have, you probably planned how you would build it. You got sand, water, and other **materials** you needed. If your plan for the castle didn't work, you changed your plan and tried again until you fixed the problem.

Engineers design

Engineers work in a similar way! Engineers are people who use math, science, and creative thinking to **design** things and solve problems. To design is to make a plan to do or build something. Engineers design many things we use every day.

Engineers design the computers we use and the houses we live in.

Finding solutions

A shovel is a **tool**. Tools are technologies that help people do work easier and faster.

Engineers find **solutions**. A solution is an answer to a question or problem. Engineers design things to solve problems. The things engineers design are called **technologies**. A technology is anything that meets a need or helps people do things. A technology is a solution to a problem.

fan

puddle

litter in a park

What do you think?

Look at the pictures on this page. Some pictures are problems. Others are technologies, or solutions. Match the correct technology to each problem.

trash can

rain boots

child on a hot day

So many solutions!

There are many problems for engineers to solve. Luckily, there are also many solutions! In fact, there is always more than one solution to a problem. The goal for engineers is finding the solution that meets the needs or solves the problem in the best possible way.

A paper fan and an electric fan both solve the problem of being hot. An electric fan, however, is a better solution for cooling more than one person.

electric fan

paper fan

Engineers improved passenger trains by designing high-speed trains. These trains can take people to places much faster than regular trains.

Making them better

Finding the best solution might mean **improving** technologies that already exist. To do this, engineers study technologies and look for problems or ways to make them better. How can trains travel faster and still be safe? How can you see your clock in the dark? Engineers look for the answers.

The design process

To help find the best solution for a problem, engineers use a set of steps known as the Engineering Design Process.

1. Find a problem
Ask questions and gather information about the problem to learn about it.

2. Brainstorm solutions
Work with a group to come up with different ideas to solve the problem.

3. Plan and make a model
As a group, choose the best solution. Create a plan to make a model of the solution. Gather materials and make your model.

4. Test and improve
Test your model. Record the results. Use the test results to help make your design better. Retest your improved design.

5. Communicate
Share your design with others.

Write on!

Engineers write all their information down in an **engineering journal**. They include why the problem needs to be solved, a list of possible solutions, their design plan, a list of materials needed, a description of how their design will be tested, the **data**, or results, from the test, and a plan for redesign.

My Engineering Journal

Brainstorming

Once engineers have found a problem and gathered all the information they can about it, it's time to look for a solution. Engineers get creative and try to think of as many solutions to a problem as they can. They **brainstorm** with others to get lots of good ideas. To brainstorm is to talk and come up with ideas in a group.

Be creative—there are no right or wrong answers! Write all the ideas in your engineering journal.

Ask questions

With so many ideas, how do engineers choose the best solution? They look carefully at each idea written in their journal. Then they think about the good and bad parts of each. They ask important questions to help them choose the best solution.

An engineer might ask questions such as "Do I have enough time and money to build it? Do I have all the tools and materials I need? Will the solution meet the needs and likely fix the problem?"

13

Test it

Engineers use **models** to test their solutions. A model is an object or drawing that shows how a technology will look and work. Models help engineers see if their designs are safe to use and if they work properly. Engineers also use models to see what changes they need to make.

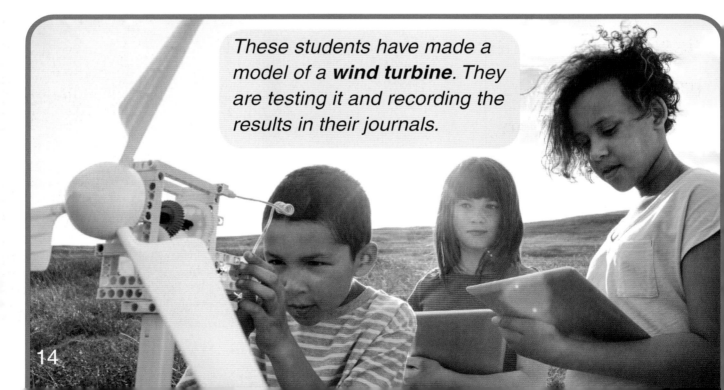

These students have made a model of a **wind turbine**. They are testing it and recording the results in their journals.

Make it better

After each test, engineers often change their design to make it better. They might change the materials or the size or shape of the design. Sometimes the solution does not work at all and engineers must start over again. They keep trying until they get it right.

If their first design doesn't work, engineers must look carefully at the problem again and choose a new solution.

Sharing solutions

Once engineers have found a solution to a problem, they share it. They **communicate** their design ideas with others. To communicate is to write, speak, or draw to share information. Sharing information helps solve the problem for others. The information may even help in finding solutions to other problems.

Engineers can use their engineering journals or models to show and explain the technologies they design to others.

Tell the world

If Thomas Edison had not shared his design of the electric light bulb, we might still be in the dark! If Alexander Graham Bell had not shared the telephone, how could we call our friends?

What do you think?

The pictures on this page show some important technologies that engineers shared with the world. What problem did each one solve?

17

Looking back

Engineers have been finding solutions to problems for thousands of years! People in **ancient** Rome, Egypt, China, and other places designed technologies to meet their needs at the time. Ancient means that they lived a long time ago.

*People in ancient Rome needed clean water for their homes and farms. Engineers designed long bridges called **aqueducts** to carry water to them.*

*Engineers in ancient Egypt designed huge buildings called **pyramids**. The Egyptians didn't leave any plans, so engineers today still do not know exactly how they were built.*

Studying the past

Today, engineers study technologies from the past. They look carefully at the designs, tools, and materials people used to solve problems. Studying the past helps engineers find solutions to today's problems. It also helps them design new technologies for the future.

Solutions in nature

Engineers also find solutions in **nature**. They study plants and animals to see how they solve problems. Then the engineers use what they learned to find solutions to people problems. For example, beavers build **dams** in streams to block the flow of water. Engineers build dams, too! These dams control the flow of water in rivers.

beaver dam

Hoover dam on the Colorado River

20

bird

Engineers study how animals find solutions to problems. Match the animals on this page with the technologies they look like!

submarine

airplane

child with flippers

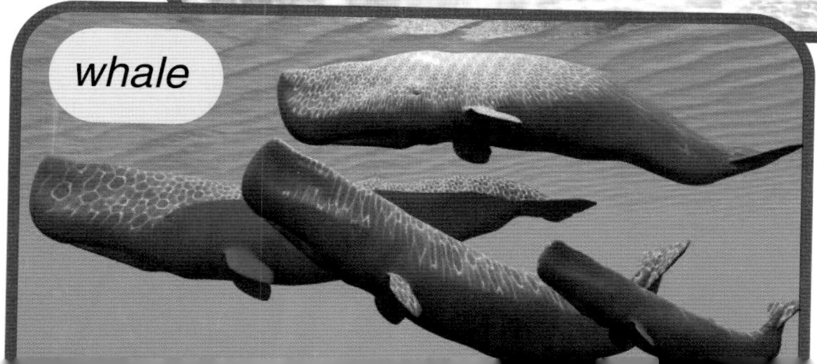

whale

duck

21

Build your own dam

Build a model of a beaver dam and then test it to see which material holds back the most water.

Materials needed:

stones

twigs

dirt

container or pan

water

1. Using a long, deep container or pan, pile the twigs in a row across the middle.

2. Pour water on one side.

Did the twigs hold back the water from reaching the other side? If not, how can you fix the dam to make it better? Build a new model using the stones and then the dirt. Which model provides the best solution for the problem?

Learning more

Books

Designing Dandelions: An Engineering Everything Adventure by
Emily Hunt and Michelle Pantoya. Texas Tech University Press, 2013.

***Engineer Through the Year: 20 Turnkey STEM Projects to Intrigue,
Inspire & Challenge (Grades K-2)*** by Sandi Reyes. Crystal Springs
Books, 2012*.*

Engineering Feats & Failures by Stephanie Paris. Teacher Created
Materials, 2013.

Engineering the ABC's: How Engineers Shape Our World by Patty
O'Brien Novak. Ferne Press, 2009.

Websites

This website provides different design activities and interactive games.
http://pbskids.org/designsquad

Discover the world of engineering with fun facts, videos, games, and much
more on this interactive website.
www.sciencekids.co.nz/engineering.html

This website shares information on how to design fun technologies.
http://pbskids.org/zoom/activities/build/

Words to know

Note: Some bolded words are defined in the text.

dam (dam) noun A barrier built in a river or stream to stop or slow down the flow of water

engineering journal (en-juh-NEER-ing JUR-nl) noun A book in which engineers write and draw problems, solutions, and models

improve (im-PROOV) *verb* To change something and make it better

material (muh-TEER-ee-uh l) noun What an object is made of

nature (NEY-cher) noun The land, plants, animals, and everything found outdoors that is not made by people

pyramid (PIR-uh-mid) noun A large building in ancient Egypt with sloping sides meeting a point and used as a tomb

technology (tek-NOL-uh-jee) noun Anything made by people that meets a need or solves a problem

wind turbine (wind TUR-bin) noun A windmill that changes wind energy into electricity

A noun is a person, place, or thing. A verb is an action word that tells you what someone or something does.

Index